SCHOLASTIC

READ & RESPOND

Bringing the best books to life in the classroom

CW00350406

Activities based on Bill's New Frock

By Anne Fine

Terms and conditions

IMPORTANT – PERMITTED USE AND WARNINGS – READ CAREFULLY BEFORE USING

This CD-ROM has been tested for viruses at all stages of its production. However, we recommend that you run virus-checking software on your computer systems at all times. Scholastic Ltd cannot accept any responsibility for any loss, disruption or damage to your data or your computer system that may occur as a result of using either the CD-ROM or the data held on it.

IF YOU ACCEPT THE ABOVE CONDITIONS YOU MAY PROCEED TO USE THE CD-ROM.

Recommended system requirements:

Windows: XP (Service Pack 3), Vista (Service Pack 2), Windows 7 or Windows 8 with 2.33GHz processor

Mac: OS 10.6 to 10.8 with Intel Core™ Duo processor

1GB RAM (recommended)

1024 x 768 Screen resolution

CD-ROM drive (24x speed recommended)

Adobe Reader (version 9 recommended for Mac users)

Broadband internet connections (for installation and updates)

For all technical support queries (including no CD drive), please phone Scholastic Customer Services on 0845 6039091.

Designed using Adobe InDesign
Scholastic Education, an imprint of Scholastic Ltd
Book End, Range Road, Witney, Oxfordshire, OX29 0YD
Registered office: Westfield Road, Southam, Warwickshire CV47 0RA

Printed and bound by Ashford Colour Press
© 2016 Scholastic Ltd
2 3 4 5 6 7 8 9   6 7 8 9 0 1 2 3 4 5

British Library Cataloguing-in-Publication Data
A catalogue record for this book is available from the British Library.
ISBN 978-1407-16060-3

Extracts from *The National Curriculum in England, English Programme of Study* © Crown Copyright. Reproduced under the terms of the Open Government Licence (OGL). http://www.nationalarchives.gov.uk/doc/open-government-licence/version/3

Due to the nature of the web, we cannot guarantee the content or links of any site mentioned. We strongly recommend that teachers check websites before using them in the classroom.

Author Pam Dowson
Editorial team Rachel Morgan, Jenny Wilcox, Emily Anderson, Gemma Cary
Series designer Neil Salt
Designer Anna Oliwa
Illustrator Adam Linley/Beehive Illustration
Digital development Hannah Barnett, Phil Crothers and MWA Technologies Private Ltd

Acknowledgements
The publishers gratefully acknowledge permission to reproduce the following copyright material:

Egmont UK for the use of the cover illustration from Bill's New Frock by Hannah Barton. Illustration copyright © Hannah Barton. Published by Egmont UK Limited and used with permission.
Egmont UK for the use of the extract from Bill's New Frock by Anne Fine, illustrated by Philippe Dupasquier. Text copyright © 1989 Anne Fine. Published by Egmont UK Limited and used with permission.

Every effort has been made to trace copyright holders for the works reproduced in this book, and the publishers apologise for any inadvertent omissions.

CONTENTS

▼ INTRODUCTION

Read & Respond provides teaching ideas related to a specific children's book. The series focuses on best-loved books and brings you ways to use them to engage your class and enthuse them about reading.

The book is divided into different sections:

- **About the book and author:** gives you some background information about the book and the author.

- **Guided reading:** breaks the book down into sections and gives notes for using it with guided reading groups. A bookmark has been provided on page 12 containing comprehension questions. The children can be directed to refer to these as they read.

- **Shared reading:** provides extracts from the children's books with associated notes for focused work. There is also one non-fiction extract that relates to the children's book.

- **Grammar, punctuation & spelling:** provides word-level work related to the children's book so you can teach grammar, punctuation and spelling in context.

- **Plot, character & setting:** contains activity ideas focused on the plot, characters and the setting of the story.

- **Talk about it:** has speaking and listening activities related to the children's book. These activities may be based directly on the children's book or be broadly based on the themes and concepts of the story.

- **Get writing:** provides writing activities related to the children's book. These activities may be based directly on the children's book or be broadly based on the themes and concepts of the story.

- **Assessment:** contains short activities that will help you assess whether the children have understood concepts and curriculum objectives. They are designed to be informal activities to feed into your planning.

The activities follow the same format:

- **Objective:** the objective for the lesson. It will be based upon a curriculum objective, but will often be more specific to the focus being covered.

- **What you need:** a list of resources you need to teach the lesson, including digital resources (printable pages, interactive activities and media resources, see page 5).

- **What to do:** the activity notes.

- **Differentiation:** this is provided where specific and useful differentiation advice can be given to support and/or extend the learning in the activity. Differentiation by providing additional adult support has not been included as this will be at a teacher's discretion based upon specific children's needs and ability, as well as the availability of support.

The activities are numbered for reference within each section and should move through the text sequentially – so you can use the lesson while you are reading the book. Once you have read the book, most of the activities can be used in any order you wish.

Below are brief guidance notes for using the CD-ROM. For more detailed information, please click on the '?' button in the top right-hand corner of the screen.

The program contains the following:
- the extract pages from the book
- all of the photocopiable pages from the book
- additional printable pages
- interactive on-screen activities
- media resources.

Getting started

Put the CD-ROM into your CD-ROM drive. If you do not have a CD-ROM drive, phone Scholastic Customer Services on 0845 6039091.

- For Windows users, the install wizard should autorun; if it fails to do so then navigate to your CD-ROM drive. Then follow the installation process.
- For Mac users, copy the disk image file to your hard drive. After it has finished copying double click it to mount the disk image. Navigate to the mounted disk image and run the installer. After installation the disk image can be unmounted and the DMG can be deleted from the hard drive.
- To install on a network, see the ReadMe file located on the CD-ROM (navigate to your drive).

To complete the installation of the program you need to open the program and click 'Update' in the pop-up. Please note – this CD-ROM is web-enabled and the content will be downloaded from the internet to your hard drive to populate the CD-ROM with the relevant resources. This only needs to be done on first use; after this you will be able to use the CD-ROM without an internet connection. If at any point any content is updated, you will receive another pop-up upon start up when there is an internet connection.

Main menu

The main menu is the first screen that appears. Here you can access: terms and conditions, registration links, how to use the CD-ROM and credits. To access a specific book click on the relevant button (note only titles installed will be available). You can filter by the

drop-down lists if you wish. You can search all resources by clicking 'Search' in the bottom left-hand corner. You can also log in and access favourites that you have bookmarked.

Resources

By clicking on a book on the Main menu, you are taken to the resources for that title. The resources are: Media, Interactives, Extracts and Printables. Select the category and then launch a resource by clicking the play button.

Teacher settings

In the top right-hand corner of the screen is a small 'T' icon. This is the teacher settings area. It is password protected; the password is: login. This area will allow you to choose the print quality settings for interactive activities ('Default' or 'Best') and also allow you to check for updates to the program or re-download all content to the disk via Refresh all content. You can also set up user logins so that you can save and access favourites. Once a user is set up, they can enter by clicking the login link underneath the 'T' and '?' buttons.

Search

You can access an all resources search by clicking the search button on the bottom left of the Main menu. You can search for activities by type (using the drop-down filter) or by keyword by typing into the box. You can then assign resources to your favourites area or launch them directly from the search area.

CURRICULUM LINKS

Section	Activity	Curriculum objectives
Guided reading		Comprehension: To develop positive attitudes to reading and an understanding of what they read.
Shared reading	1	Comprehension: To participate in discussion about both books that are read to them and those they can read for themselves, taking turns and listening to what others say.
	2	Comprehension: To identify how language, structure and presentation contribute to meaning.
	3	Comprehension: To identify how language, structure and presentation contribute to meaning.
	4	Comprehension: To retrieve and record information from non-fiction.
Grammar, punctuation & spelling	1	Composition: To use word families based on common words.
	2	Composition: To draft and write by organising paragraphs around a theme.
	3	Composition: To use and punctuate direct speech.
	4	Composition: To use the forms 'a' or 'an' according to whether the next word begins with a consonant or a vowel.
	5	Transcription: To use suffixes and understand how to add them.
	6	Transcription: To use suffixes and understand how to add them.
Plot, character & setting	1	Comprehension: To identify main ideas drawn from more than one paragraph and summarise them.
	2	Comprehension: To draw inferences such as inferring characters' feelings, thoughts and motives from their actions, and justify inferences with evidence.
	3	Comprehension: To identify main ideas drawn from more than one paragraph and summarise them.
	4	Comprehension: To draw inferences such as inferring characters' feelings, thoughts and motives from their actions, and justify inferences with evidence.
	5	Comprehension: To identify main ideas drawn from more than one paragraph and summarise them.
	6	Comprehension: To identify main ideas drawn from more than one paragraph and summarise them.
	7	Comprehension: To draw inferences such as inferring characters' feelings, thoughts and motives from their actions, and justify inferences with evidence.
	8	Comprehension: To identify themes.

Section	Activity	Curriculum objectives
Talk about it	1	Spoken language: To consider and evaluate different viewpoints, attending to and building on the contributions of others.
	2	Spoken language: To participate in debates.
	3	Spoken language: To participate in improvisations.
	4	Spoken language: To articulate and justify answers, arguments and opinions.
	5	Spoken language: To use spoken language to develop understanding through exploring ideas.
	6	Spoken language: To ask relevant questions to extend their understanding and knowledge.
Get writing	1	Composition: To discuss writing similar to that which they are planning to write in order to understand and learn from its structure, vocabulary and grammar.
	2	Composition: To draft and write by creating settings, characters and plot in narratives.
	3	Composition: To draft and write by creating settings, characters and plot in narratives.
	4	Composition: To compose and rehearse sentences orally, progressively building a varied and rich vocabulary and an increasing range of sentence structures.
	5	Composition: To draft and write by creating settings, characters and plot in narratives.
	6	Composition: To use simple organisational devices, such as headings and sub-headings, in non-narrative material.
Assessment	1	Composition: To draft and write by organising paragraphs around a theme.
	2	Composition: To use simple organisational devices, such as headings and subheadings, in non-narrative material.
	3	Comprehension: To draw inferences such as inferring characters' feelings, thoughts and motives from their actions, and justify inferences with evidence.
	4	Comprehension: To identify main ideas drawn from more than one paragraph and summarise these.
	5	Composition: To draft and write by organising paragraphs around a theme.
	6	Composition: To use and punctuate direct speech.

BILL'S NEW FROCK

About the book

Bill's New Frock tells of a day in the life of Bill Simpson, who wakes up one morning to find, to his horror, that he has apparently changed into a girl, and to make matters worse his mother brings him a pretty frilly frock to wear. With no time to ask questions, Bill has to go off to school in his new frock and discover what life is like when you are no longer a boy but have suddenly and inexplicably become a girl. Everyone he meets treats him differently from usual, from the bully on the corner to his classmates and the school staff. People speak to him differently, using different language, and have different expectations of his behaviour and abilities. Using humour to explore the theme of gender inequality from an individual's perspective, the book raises many questions pertinent to today's society. Should boys and girls be treated differently? Is it fair? Should we have different expectations for people, based on their gender alone? To Bill's relief, his life as a female is short-lived as he once again dons his usual jeans and shirt, but it is likely that his attitudes will have changed forever.

About the author

Anne Fine was born in Leicester in 1947. She enjoyed writing stories at school, but never thought about becoming a writer. She studied Politics and History at Warwick University and became a secondary-school teacher, afterwards working as an information officer for the charity Oxfam. When she married she lived in several parts of the United States and Canada before finally settling in County Durham in the UK. She has two daughters. It was only when she was snowed in one winter and unable to get to the library to change her books that she first sat down to write a novel of her own. Since then she has written dozens of books, mostly for children but also a few for adults, and has won many awards including the Carnegie Medal in 1989 and 1992 and the Guardian Fiction Award in 1990. She was the Children's Laureate from 2001 to 2003.

About the illustrator

Philippe Dupasquier was born in Switzerland in 1955. He has illustrated many books, both of his own and for others. His detailed comic book style adds much to stories, and he has used it to good effect in wordless picture books such as *Dear Daddy* and *A Country Far Away*. He won the Smarties Prize and was commended for the Carnegie Medal for his illustrations for *Bill's New Frock*.

Key facts

Bill's New Frock

Author: Anne Fine

Illustrator: Philippe Dupasquier

First published: 1989 by Methuen Children's Books

Awards: Nestlé Smarties Book Prize for 6–8 year olds in 1990, highly commended for the Carnegie Medal in 1990, winner of the Nottinghamshire Libraries Award in 1990 and winner of the Leicestershire Children's Book Prize in 2012.

Did you know? Anne Fine got the idea for the book when her children moved from school in the USA to school in the UK and noticed a big difference in the way boys and girls were treated. In the USA they were treated equally, but in the UK there were huge differences. A TV adaptation of the book was broadcast in 1998. It is also available as an audio book and an ebook.

Chapter 1

Look together at the cover of the book. Ask: *What is unexpected about the title?* Do the children know any other books by Anne Fine? Read the opening, up to 'This cannot be true!'. Ask: *How might Bill feel and what might he think when he discovers he has become a girl?* Using question 6 on the Guided Reading bookmark (page 12), ask the children to make a note of any language that is particularly girlish in nature ('dear', 'poppet', 'sweet', 'pretty', 'girls are neater'). Read on to 'Mean Malcolm in his purple studded jacket', referring to question 10 on the bookmark about clothes reflecting character. As they read the rest of the chapter, ask the children to consider question 1 on the Guided Reading bookmark, noting examples of how people react differently to Bill because he is a girl, such as the head teacher, the old lady, the teacher telling him not to dirty his clothes and his neat writing not being neat enough. Continue reading up to 'subject was closed, rather sharply'. What do the children think about Astrid's complaint that boys are always chosen instead of girls to move the tables? Read on to 'salwar kameez'. How do we know from this section that there is no school uniform? Would the story be different if there had been one? As they read the section about Bill's and Philip's handwriting, up to 'thumping Philip', what are the children's reactions? Read on to the end of the chapter. Have they noticed that no one seems to see any difference in Bill? Ask: *Why hasn't Bill told anyone about what has happened?* Go over the notes they have made while reading, discussing their observations. Ask the children how they would have reacted in Bill's situation.

Chapter 2

Discuss the chapter title. Does anyone have any ideas what it might be? Read up to 'see the squares any longer' and ask the children to consider question 2 on the Guided Reading bookmark about playground demarcation. Discuss their thoughts. Remind the children that the book was written in 1989. Do they think playgrounds are the same today, or have there been any changes? Read on to 'fur had gone all browny-yellow'. Do the children have any more ideas about what a 'wumpy choo' might be now? Continue reading to 'Go *round*!'. Ask the children's opinions about the boys welcoming other boys to their game but saying that girls get in the way. Read on to '*every single bit* of the playground!'. Ask: *Who seems to be in charge here? Why should that be?* Refer to question 4 on the bookmark, explaining that italics have been used for emphasis. Ask: *What words could you use to describe Bill's actions in arguing with the group of boys?* (brave, confident, fearless) Read to the end of the chapter, where they discover what a 'wumpy choo' is. Did anyone work it out? Discuss the difficulty of interpreting words you hear when learning a new language. Do any of the children have any experience of mishearing words, perhaps in song lyrics?

Chapter 3

As they read up to 'Pink, pink, nothing but pink!', ask the children to focus on question 7 on the Guided Reading bookmark, about the way dialogue is reported. Share their observations, inviting them to read the dialogue section aloud, using appropriate intonation. Read together the next paragraph, up to 'that's all pink?'. What do they notice about the things Kirsty mentions? (They are not 'girly'.) Continue reading up to 'off his paint tub'. Ask: *Was the teacher right to insist that Bill should be the model?* Ask them to justify their opinions. Focus on the following three paragraphs, ending with 'What next?'. Do they notice how an event that would have happened quickly has been described in detail, slowing it down? Why is this effective? (It enables us to visualise the whole accident; gives us more idea of how Bill and the others would feel.) As they read to the end of the chapter, ask the children to consider question 11 on the bookmark, about Bill's feelings, discussing their thoughts afterwards. Ask the children how they would feel to be chosen. Bill is embarrassed, but might there be other occasions when he would feel pleased or flattered? What makes the difference?

Chapter 4

Read up to 'scuttled hastily into the GIRLS'. Discuss Bill's dilemma about choosing which toilet to go into. What would the children have done? Continue reading up to 'hurried off'. Ask the children to predict what might happen next. Read on to 'How *can* you?', referring again to question 4 on the Guided Reading bookmark, about the use of italics for emphasis. Can the children answer Bill's question here – 'How can you *live* without pockets?'. As they read on, stopping at 'sweet little frock!', ask the children to consider question 12 on the bookmark, discussing their thoughts on the adults' behaviour towards Bill. Read together the paragraph starting 'It wasn't Bill's fault'. Do they notice how the author has again used the technique of detailing an incident that happened quickly, thus slowing down the pace? When they have read to the end of the chapter, refer to question 3 on the bookmark, discussing the children's ideas about how Bill might have prevented dropping everything. Why didn't he ask for help? This is another example of Bill accepting his situation and not trying to explain that something unusual has happened to him. Ask the children what this tells us about Bill's character. Is he shy? Embarrassed? Confused? Does he seem worried that this change could be permanent? Do they think he has even considered that possibility?

Chapter 5

Ask the children to read the opening of the chapter up to 'at the very least, quiet', considering question 8 on the Guided Reading bookmark about language use. This is a good example of the use of pathetic fallacy, where the teacher's mood echoes the weather. (They do not need to know the term.) Ask: *How does this device make the writing more interesting?* (It makes the description of both weather and teacher's mood stronger; it holds our attention.) As they read on to 'given that to Rohan', ask the children to make a note of the comic names mentioned. Can they sort their list into comics for boys and comics for girls? How did they decide? Do they recognise any of the titles? (Some are no longer published.) Ask the children to read on to 'shadow fell over the page'. Are they surprised by the stories in Bill's copy of *Bunty*? Would they expect the stories in boys' and girls' comics to be different? Are books divided into boys/girls? Is it important? As they read on, pause at the phrase 'The penny dropped'. Do they know its meaning? If not, can they work it out from the context? When they have finished the chapter, discuss the fight. Was it justified? Could it have been avoided? Note the use of the words '*angry*' and '*upset*' at the end, and their gender bias.

Chapter 6

As they read the opening pages, up to 'work books', ask the children to focus on question 9 on the Guided Reading bookmark, noting the verbs used. Talk about the author's choices, such as 'sailed', 'blazed', 'steamed', 'reflected', 'astonished', 'ignored' 'slid', 'spilled', 'overlooked' and 'imprisoned'. Agree that they add to the interest for the reader, and have been deliberately chosen over simpler, less effective verbs. Read on to 'So everyone stood in line'. Ask:

Why do you think the teacher organised the races in the ways that she did? (To try and make them fairer.) Read the next short section up to 'I won my heat!', where Paul runs on his own. Ask: *How do you think Paul would feel about not racing against anybody? Could the teacher have done anything else to help him feel included?* (Note: If you have disabled children in your class, treat this sensitively.) Read on to 'let him win the race', where the girls plan for Paul to win. Ask: *What do you think about the girls' plan?* Carry on reading the description of the race, pausing at 'He couldn't let Paul win'. Can the children predict what will happen in the rest of the race? Read on to 'He'd *won!*' and ask the children to explain what they liked about the way the race was described, choosing sections they thought were particularly effective and explaining their choice. When they have read to the end of the chapter, ask them to consider question 13 on the bookmark, reflecting on Bill's approach to the race. What might the girls think of Bill afterwards? You could extend this discussion to ask the children to find out about Paralympic sport, something that was uncommon at the time the book was written.

encounter with Mean Malcolm, up to 'and saw him'. This is Bill's second fight of the day. What does it tell us about him? Do the children think he always fights? What might Malcolm feel about a girl reacting to him in this way? After they have read to the end of the chapter, ask the children to consider question 5 on the Guided Reading bookmark and discuss their thoughts about the action taking place on just one day. Do they think Bill might treat girls – and boys – any differently after his experiences? Would he ever tell anyone what had happened to him? If he did, what might people's reactions be? Would different people react differently? For example, Bill's parents, his friends, his teachers. What do the children think would happen when Bill went to school the next day?

Chapter 7

Ask the children to read up to 'old self tomorrow!', noting the use of 'you're your' and asking them to explain the difference in the homophones. How do they remember which to use? Read the following paragraph, up to 'not to see', drawing attention to the words 'dispirited', 'trailed' and 'dragging', used to describe Bill, and 'jumping' and 'excitedly', used to describe Paul, comparing them. Talk about how careful word choice shows rather than tells us how a character is feeling, making the writing stronger and more interesting. Continue reading about Bill's

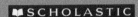

READ & RESPOND

Bringing the best books to life in the classroom

Bill's New Frock
by Anne Fine

Focus on...
Meaning

1. In what ways do people react differently to Bill as a girl?

2. Why might the playground be divided between boys and girls? What do you think about this?

3. What might Bill have done to make his trip to the office easier?

Focus on...
Organisation

4. How have italics been used in this section?

5. Why might the author have chosen to limit Bill's experiences to just one day? How does this decision impact on the story?

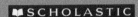

READ & RESPOND

Bringing the best books to life in the classroom

Bill's New Frock
by Anne Fine

Focus on...
Language and features

6. Pick out language in this chapter that is more to do with girls than boys.

7. How do we know who is speaking, and how does this affect the pace of the story?

8. In the opening to this chapter, how does the description of the weather link to the teacher's mood?

9. Note the verbs used in the opening of the chapter. Have they been used effectively?

Focus on...
Purpose, viewpoints and effects

10. How do the clothes Bill and Malcolm are wearing link to their gender? What do they tell us about the characters?

11. How might Bill feel when chosen to be the subject of the art class because of his pink dress?

12. How do the adults behave towards Bill when asking him to take things to the office?

13. Does Bill behave more like a boy by not letting Paul win the race?

Extract 1

- Display Extract 1, which is from the opening pages of the book. Allow the children to read it silently before reading it aloud for them. Ask for their immediate impressions. What do they think about Bill's discovery? Can they ascertain something of the personalities of Bill, Mum and Dad from what they say and do?

- Read again the opening sentence. Can the children suggest why Anne Fine chose to start the story in this direct way? (For example: it takes us straight to the heart of the story; it has some surprise value that makes us want to keep reading.)

- Highlight the words 'still standing staring', explaining the alliteration here.

- Underline the italicised word *'never'*, inviting the children to suggest how this should be read. Read it both with and without emphasis, demonstrating the difference.

- Circle the words 'baffled', 'astonishment', 'dismay', 'scowl' and 'muttered savagely'. Ask: *What do these words tell us about Bill's mood and feelings?* Can the children suggest antonyms that would convey an opposite set of reactions?

- Draw attention to Mum and Dad's interactions with Bill. Do they seem surprised that Bill is now a girl? Discuss their language use, and its feminine bias. Ask for examples, highlighting the children's choices.

- Point out the way speech is set out and punctuated, using speech marks and a separate line for each new speaker. Ask: *How does this punctuation help us to understand what we are reading?*

Extract 2

- Display Extract 2, from Chapter 4, and invite individuals to read the first word. Ask: *Is this a sentence?* Agree that it isn't, as it does not contain a verb. Ask why the author has written this way; what impact does it have? Read the following sentence, noting its length compared with the preceding word.

- Allow the children to read through the whole extract silently, to get a sense of the piece, and then refer to the paragraph beginning 'No'. What do they notice about sentence length here? Is it effective? Explain that several short sentences are balanced by the longer one describing the dress.

- Underline the word 'But', used as a sentence opener in this paragraph. Explain that we do not usually use the word in this way. Why does it work in this instance? Can they spot the other sentence where it is used similarly?

- Highlight the repeated phrase 'imitation lace'. Explain that we can tell the author has deliberately used repetition here to strengthen the writing, emphasising the object.

- Invite a child to come to the board and highlight the alliteration in the paragraph that begins 'Then he felt' ('pretty', 'pink', 'pocket').

- Ask them to count the questions, inviting a child to come to the board and highlight the question marks. Discuss why there are so many questions, and their impact on the story.

- Ask: *How can we tell that Bill thinks it's ridiculous not to have pockets in a dress?*

Extract 3

- Display and read Extract 3, which is taken from Chapter 5. Ask the children which senses describe the weather. (Sight and hearing.) Highlight the words 'gunfire' and 'pinging'. Ask: *Why might the author have chosen these two words?*

- Invite the children to compare the weather with the description in the next paragraph of Mrs Collins' mood. Explain that writers use this device of linking the weather with characters or events to make the writing stronger. Do they think it is effective?

- Underline 'her lips thinning into tightened purse strings'. Explain this description of the teacher's mouth is an indication of her mood. Some children may like to know this is called a metaphor.

- Read up to 'quiet'. Invite the children to find words to do with sound. Highlight their choices ('beat heavily', 'crept quietly', 'quiet'). Point out that the weather contrasts with the children's behaviour.

- Read to the end of the extract. Do they notice anything unusual about the tenses here? Underline 'dip', 'pick', 'pushing', 'shoving' and 'using'. Ask the children the tense of these verbs (present). Invite them to identify any verbs written in the past tense.

- Highlight the first sentence of the last paragraph. Invite the children to suggest another way this might have been written (such as 'Everybody made a great noise and a fuss.'). Ask: *Which of the two is more effective, and why?*

- Underline each instance of the word *'meant'*. Invite the children to read out the sentences that include it, using appropriate emphasis.

Extract 4

- Display Extract 4 and ask the children to read it through silently to themselves. Afterwards, ask for their reactions to the information about boys wearing dresses and discuss their responses. Display the media resource '18th-century children' to aid discussion.

- Ask: *What three reasons are given for young boys wearing dresses?* Highlight the answers in paragraph two. Ask: *How would you be able to distinguish between boys and girls when they were dressed the same?* Again, highlight the answer.

- Ask: *What was breeching and why was it called that?* Highlight the relevant section in paragraph three. Ask: *What clothes would the boys wear once they stopped wearing dresses?* Highlight the answers in paragraph four.

- Invite the children to offer their opinions about how the boys would have felt at that time about wearing dresses, discussing their thoughts.

- Underline the sentence in paragraph three about working-class boys going to work. Do the children notice anything unusual about this fact? Do they know anything about child labour in history?

- Ask: *How do we know that boys used to wear dresses?* (From paintings and letters.)

- Circle the word 'assumed' in paragraph one. Do the children know its meaning or can they deduce it from the context? Repeat with 'graduated' in paragraph three.

- Can the children suggest why the tradition of boys wearing dresses might have died out?

Extract 1

Chapter 1

When Bill Simpson woke up on Monday morning, he found he was a girl.

He was still standing staring at himself in the mirror, quite baffled, when his mother swept in.

'Why don't you wear this pretty pink dress?' she said.

'I *never* wear dresses,' Bill burst out.

'I know,' his mother said. 'It's such a pity.'

And, to his astonishment, before he could even begin to argue, she had dropped the dress over his head and zipped up the back.

'I'll leave you to do up the shell buttons,' she said. 'They're a bit fiddly and I'm late for work.'

And she swept out, leaving him staring in dismay at the mirror. In it, a girl with his curly red hair and wearing a pretty pink frock with fiddly shell buttons was staring back at him in equal dismay.

'This can't be true,' Bill Simpson said to himself. 'This cannot be true!'

He stepped out of his bedroom just as his father was rushing past. He, too, was late in getting off to work.

Mr Simpson leaned over and planted a kiss on Bill's cheek.

'Bye, Poppet,' he said, ruffling Bill's curls. 'You look very sweet today. It's not often we see you in a frock, is it?'

He ran down the stairs and out of the house so quickly he didn't see Bill's scowl, or hear what he muttered savagely under his breath.

Extract 2

Chapter 4

Pockets?

Carefully, Bill squatted in the corridor and lowered the pile of yellow medical forms to the floor, taking care that he didn't lose the key or drop the little glass bottles of coloured ink.

Then he felt all round the pretty pink frock for a pocket. He pushed and shoved at frilly places here and there, wherever he thought one might be hidden. But though he heard the material rip once or twice, and felt his hands go through the holes he'd accidentally torn, there were no pockets there.

No. Not one pocket. Acres of material. Masses of it. Pleats, frills, bows, scallops, fancy loops. But not one pocket. Whoever designed the dress had gone to all the trouble of matching the imitation lace round the hem with the imitation lace round the collar, and fitting a zip in so neatly that it was practically invisible, and putting comfortable elastic around the little puffy sleeves.

But they just hadn't bothered to put in a pocket.

Bill was *amazed*. How was a person in a frock like this supposed to *survive*? How were they expected to get along without any pockets? It can't have been the only dress of its kind that was made. Other people must wear them. Where did they put their money, for heaven's sake? Did they keep it, all damp and hot and sticky, in the palms of their hands all day? Where did they put the sweets their friends gave them if they wanted to save them for later? What did they do if someone returned their pencil sharpener to them outside in break?

How can you *live* without pockets? How can you? How *can* you?

Extract 3

Chapter 5

It rained all through the lunch hour. The sky went grey, the windows misted over, and from overhead came the steady gunfire sound of huge raindrops pinging smartly on the skylight.

And Mrs Collins slipped into one of her dark wet-break moods.

Everyone knew the signs: the eyebrows knitting together over her nose; the lines across her forehead deepening to furrows; her lips thinning into tightened purse strings.

Everyone knew it was not the time to cause trouble.

So as the rain beat heavily against the window panes, everyone crept quietly around the classroom, trying to look as if they were up to something useful or sensible, or, at the very least, quiet.

And out of the storeroom came the old comic box.

Nobody *meant* to make a great noise and a fuss. All anyone wanted was simply to go to the box, dip in their hand, and pick out a couple of comics they liked. Nobody *meant* to end up in a scrum, pushing and shoving the others out of the way, using their elbows, desperate to get an arm in and whip out a favourite comic before someone else leaned over and snatched it.

Nobody *meant* to end up in a riot.

Extract 4

Have you ever seen an old oil painting of a wealthy family, and assumed that all the children in it were girls? Well, you may have been mistaken, because for more than 300 years, from the mid-16th to the late 19th century, it was usual for both boys and girls to wear dresses.

Up to the age of about seven, boys wore frocks just like their sisters. There were several reasons for this: it was easier for them to use the toilet (this was before the invention of zips!); it was easier to alter a dress to fit as the boy grew; and in poor households boys could wear their older sisters' hand-me-downs. Often the colours of boys' and girls' clothes helped to distinguish them, with boys wearing darker colours and girls wearing paler shades.

When a boy graduated to the wearing of trousers, this was known as 'breeching', because trousers then were called breeches. This was an important time for the boy and his family as it was a sign that he was growing up. Some families even had a special ceremony, marking the occasion. For working-class boys it often meant they could now go out to work without a dress getting in the way. Historians have studied letters written throughout the period, where mothers describe their preparations for their sons' move into trousers, and their feelings about it.

At different times in history a boy's new clothing might include at first a short dress, rather than the ankle-length one worn earlier, a short jacket or, in the 19th century, short trousers. Boys' and girls' hair was also different once they were past toddlerhood. Boys might still have longish hair, but girls' hair would be longer and often worn tied up, like their mothers.

GRAMMAR, PUNCTUATION & SPELLING

1. Word families

To use word families based on common words.

Photocopiable page 22 'Word families', interactive activity 'Find the relatives'.

What to do

- On the board, write the word 'manage'. Invite the children to suggest other words they know that use 'manage' as their base. They may suggest 'manager', 'managing', 'management', 'managed', 'manageable', 'unmanageable' and 'mismanage'. Scribe their suggestions on the board, ensuring they know the meanings.

- Explain that there are many words that are grouped together in families, where meaning and spelling are linked. This is more than the different tenses of verbs, although verbs may be included, as in 'manage'.

- Work through the interactive activity 'Find the relatives' with the class, or allow them to do this independently.

- Hand out photocopiable page 22 'Word families' for the children to complete independently. As they complete the task, ask them to find a partner and compare their answers, making any changes they think necessary after comparison and discussion.

- Draw the class together to review the photocopiable task. Can anyone think of other words to add to the families on the sheet, such as 'reaction', 'dissolution', 'actress', 'dissolved', 'enact'?

Support: Ask the children to underline the words they are familiar with. Of those left, invite them to choose one or two at a time to learn their meaning and spelling, focusing on the base words each time to help them.
Extension: Challenge the children to seek out other word families, adding them in groups to their spelling journals.

2. Introduction to paragraphs

To introduce paragraphs as a way to group related material.

Copies of *Bill's New Frock* or the children's own current reading book, photocopiable page 23 'Using paragraphs', interactive activity 'Paragraph planning'.

What to do

- Ask the children to open any page of their reading book or copy of *Bill's New Frock*. What do they notice about how the text is set out? Discuss their responses, focusing on the use of paragraphs. Explain that paragraphs are used to group together sentences that are linked in meaning or context. Setting text out this way makes it easier to read.

- Display interactive activity 'Paragraph planning'. Explain that the notes are mixed up and need sorting into those that would logically go together to make two paragraphs in total. Allow the children a few minutes to discuss with a partner how they would organise the notes before taking suggestions from the class to complete the boxes on screen.

- Hand out photocopiable page 23 'Using paragraphs'. Draw attention to the solid block of text, explaining that it needs to be paragraphed. Ask the children to read it through twice before marking it to show where they would make paragraph divisions. They should then continue to write their own short paragraphed piece on the back of the sheet. They can make brief notes first if they wish.

Support: Instead of their own piece, the children can write the paragraphs resulting from the interactive activity.

3. Using speech marks

Objective

To introduce the use of inverted commas to punctuate direct speech.

What you need

Photocopiable page 24 'Using speech marks', Extract 1, media resource 'Speech bubbles'.

What to do

- Display Extract 1. Invite children to come to the board and underline any of the dialogue, each choosing one speech. Ask: *How do you know these are spoken words?* (The speech marks and words such as 'she said' are the clues.) If they don't notice, point out that there is a new line for each new piece of speech. Explain that these devices make reading the text easier, helping comprehension. Explain that we use the terms 'speech marks' or 'inverted commas', and they act rather like a mouth opening and closing around the spoken words.

- Display media resource 'Speech bubbles'. Invite the children to suggest names for the two runners. Demonstrate how to rewrite the spoken words from the speech bubbles using speech marks and the names they have suggested, to show who is speaking.

- Hand out photocopiable page 24 'Using speech marks', for the children to complete independently.

- Allow the children to compare their choice of speeches with a partner, also checking each other's punctuation.

Differentiation

Support: Allow them to just complete the speech bubbles on the photocopiable sheet, until they are more familiar with distinguishing the spoken word.

Extension: Encourage the children to give each speaker two sentences to say, using, for example, 'said Bill' between them, rather than at the end. Invite them to use alternative verbs to 'said' to add more interest.

4. A or an?

Objective

To use the forms 'a' or 'an' according to whether the next word begins with a consonant or a vowel.

What you need

Printable page 'A or an?', interactive activity 'A or an?'.

What to do

- Ensure the children are confident in their knowledge of vowels and consonants.

- Explain the rule: we use 'a' before a word that begins with a consonant and 'an' before a word that begins with a vowel. To demonstrate, write on the board 'apricot', 'dog', 'chair', 'owl', 'yacht', 'elf', 'icicle' and 'guitar'. Ask the children to identify the words beginning with vowels and invite individuals to come to the board and write 'a' or 'an' in front of each word.

- Work through interactive activity 'A or an?' with the class, or allow the children to complete it independently.

- Hand out printable page 'A or an?' for the children to complete independently.

Differentiation

Support: Ask the children to write the words from the interactive activity on to individual cards. With a partner, they should place the cards face down on the table, taking turns to choose a card and saying whether it would be preceded by 'a' or 'an'. If their partner agrees, they win the card. Continue until all cards are used and there is a winner.

Extension: Challenge the children to create further phrases similar to those on the printable page, where the adjective is the word needing 'a' or 'an'.

Sounds like /shun/

Objective

To use endings that sound like /shun/ – 'tion', 'sion', 'ssion' and 'cian'.

What you need

Printable page 'Sounds like /shun/', dictionaries.

What to do

Write on the board the endings 'tion', 'sion', 'ssion' and 'cian'. Ask the children to read them aloud and agree they all make the sound /shun/. Explain that because they all sound the same, we have to remember what they look like in terms of spelling.

On the board, write 'imitacian', 'imitation' and 'imitasion'. Ask the children to choose the correct spelling, write it on their individual whiteboards and show you. Rub out the two incorrect spellings for the children to check their choices.

Repeat with other words, such as 'discussion', 'exhaustion', 'mathematician' and 'tension', offering alternative spellings each time for the children to choose from.

Hand out printable page 'Sounds like /shun/' for the children to complete independently.

Differentiation

Support: Allow the children to omit any sections of the sheet they feel unsure about. Use that information to plan future work.
Extension: On the reverse of the sheet, challenge the children to create four lists of words, one for each ending. Allow them to use dictionaries, either paper or online, to research their words.

6. The suffix 'ous'

Objective

To use the suffix 'ous'.

What you need

Interactive activity 'The suffix 'ous''.

What to do

- On the board, write the words 'glorious', 'famous', 'curious', 'jealous' and 'serious'. Ask the children what the words have in common, agreeing they all have the 'ous' ending and they are all adjectives. Draw attention to the use of the letter 'i' in 'glorious', 'curious' and 'serious'. (Some children may mistakenly think it could be a letter 'y'.) Add the suffix 'ly' to each word. Ask: *What type of words are they now?* (adverbs)

- Display interactive activity 'The suffix 'ous'' and work through it with the children.

- Give the children the following words to write on their individual whiteboards, and ask them to show you each one: 'furious', 'tremendous', 'generous', 'glorious', 'previous', 'tedious' and 'glamorous'. Write the correct spelling for each word afterwards for the children to check their work.

- On the board write the word 'fame', demonstrating how it loses its final letter when 'ous' is added. Ask the children to write on their individual whiteboards the 'ous' words made from these root words: 'adventure', 'chivalry', 'continue' and 'nerve'.

- Challenge the children to create the 'ous' words from these root words: 'caution', 'disaster', 'envy', 'hilarity', 'luxury'.

Differentiation

Support: Allow the children to repeat the interactive activity independently or with a partner to gain extra confidence.
Extension: Challenge the children to keep a list in their spelling journals of words they encounter with the 'ous' ending.

Word families

● Choose words from the word bank below to complete the four word families.

solve

_____

_____

_____

_____

_____

_____

_____

use

_____

_____

_____

_____

_____

_____

_____

family

_____

_____

_____

_____

_____

_____

_____

_____

act

_____

_____

_____

_____

_____

_____

dissolve	inactive	react	misuse
familiar	useful	activity	familiarise
actor	disused	action	useless
unfamiliar	interact	solution	insoluble
active	familiarity	solver	interact

Using paragraphs

Put marks like this **//** to show where you would divide this piece into paragraphs.

The story of *Bill's New Frock* is about a boy called Bill who wakes up one morning to discover that he has changed into a girl. Bill is surprised and confused and has no idea how it happened. His mum gives him a pretty pink frock to wear. On his way to school Bill meets Mean Malcolm, the bully. He expects him to cause trouble but Malcolm just whistles as Bill passes. Further on he meets an old lady who helps him across the road.

When he arrives at school the headmaster is someone else who doesn't seem to see any change in him. Bill notices that the head doesn't tell him off like he does to the boys. As the day goes on Bill gets into all sorts of difficulties. He seems to find life full of problems now that he is a girl. On the way back home, Bill once again bumps into Mean Malcolm who whistles at him again. By now Bill has had enough and fights the bully, leaving him sprawling on the ground. When he gets back home, Bill returns to being a boy, much to his relief.

On the back of the sheet, write a short piece about one of your own days at school. Choose three or four separate incidents, writing one short paragraph for each.

Using speech marks

● From what you know of them in the story *Bill's New Frock*, think of something that each of these characters might say. Write their words in the speech bubbles.

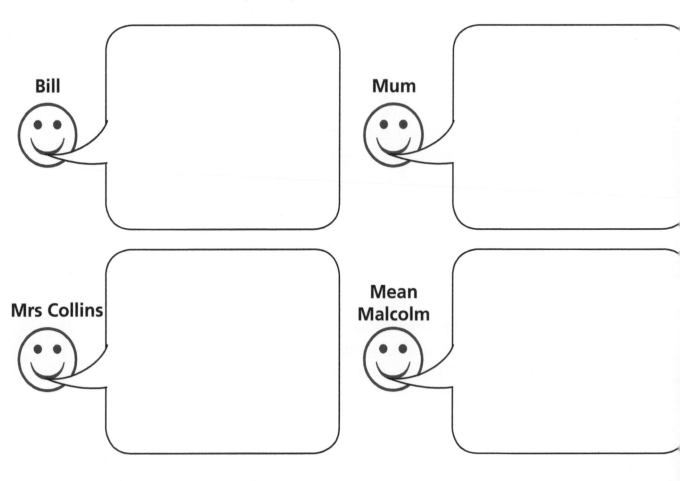

● Now rewrite their words, using speech marks and indicating who has spoken.

_____

_____

_____

_____

_____

_____

_____

PLOT, CHARACTER & SETTING

1. Boy becomes girl!

Objective
To identify main ideas drawn from more than one paragraph and summarise them.

What you need
Photocopiable page 29 'What do you think?'.

Cross-curricular link
PSHE

What to do
- Ensure the children have read Chapter 1 of *Bill's New Frock* before the lesson.

- Agree that no one notices the difference in Bill. Ask: *Why do you think the author has done this? How would the story have been different if they had? Would it have been the same if it was a girl changing to a boy?* Discuss the children's responses.

- Hand out photocopiable page 29 'What do you think' for the children to complete independently. As they finish, allow them to compare and discuss their thoughts with a partner.

- When everyone has completed the sheet, bring the class together to discuss the children's various responses to the sentence-completion section of the sheet.

- Invite the children to share the words they chose to describe Bill's feelings in the second section of the sheet, writing them on the board. Can any of the words be used for more than one of the scenarios presented?

Differentiation
Support: Allow the children to work in pairs to complete the photocopiable sheet.
Extension: Invite the children to write a summary of the opening chapter, using paragraphs.

2. Drawing inferences

Objective
To draw inferences such as characters' feelings, thoughts and motives from their actions and justify with evidence.

What you need
Copy of *Bill's New Frock*, photocopiable page 30 'How did Bill feel?', individual whiteboards.

Cross-curricular link
PSHE

What to do
- Read aloud the section in Chapter 1 about the handwriting lesson, from 'He wrote more' to 'The Lovely Rapunzel'.

- Invite the children's ideas about Bill's feelings in this section, discussing their responses. Do they think this is representative of boys' and girls' handwriting? Ask: *Why do you think Bill wrote more neatly than usual? Was it his decision or was it something that came with being a girl?*

- Allow the children a few minutes to talk with a partner, choosing words to describe Bill's feelings throughout the lesson and writing their choices on their individual whiteboards.

- Invite them to share their words, listing them on the board and discussing their appropriateness.

- Hand out photocopiable page 30 'How did Bill feel?' for the children to complete independently, noting whether any of the words on the sheet were chosen earlier by the children.

Differentiation
Support: Ensure the children know the meanings of the words 'outraged' and 'dismayed' on the photocopiable sheet. If they are confused by the words, allow them to omit these two sentences.
Extension: Encourage the children to include the word 'because' in their sentences on the photocopiable sheet.

3. The playground

Objective

To identify main ideas drawn from more than one paragraph and summarise them.

What you need

Copy of *Bill's New Frock*, three large sheets of sugar paper, sticky notes, printable page 'Playground rules'.

Cross-curricular link

PSHE

What to do

- Read aloud from Chapter 2 the paragraph beginning 'Each boy who ran'. Ask: *Who seems to be in charge of this set-up? How can you tell?*

- Read aloud from 'He walked towards the footballers' to '*every single bit* of the playground!'. Ask: *Is this fair?* Encourage the children to justify their opinions.

- Arrange the class into mixed-ability groups of 4–6 children. Ask each group to talk about what happens in their playground, listing their observations on sticky notes and posting them on the large sheets of paper on the wall, under the headings 'Boys', 'Girls' and 'Anybody'. You may wish to limit the children to six sticky notes per group. When they have finished, discuss the results.

- Hand out printable page 'Playground rules' for pairs of children to complete. Display their completed ideas to stimulate further discussion.

Differentiation

Support: Allow the children to just draw the plan on the reverse of the sheet, rather than completing the tasks on the front.
Extension: Encourage the children to give reasons for their rules on the printable sheet.

4. It happened at school

Objective

To draw inferences such as characters' feelings, thoughts and motives from their actions and justify with evidence.

What you need

Interactive activity 'Choose the setting'.

What to do

- Ensure the children have read the story *Bill's New Frock* before the lesson.

- Ask the children what settings they can recall from any part of the story.

- Display interactive activity 'Choose the setting', and work through it with the class. When complete, ask: *Where does most of the action of the story take place?* Agree it is mostly set at school. Ask: *Why is it important for the story to be set on a school day?* (There are more people who know Bill, more chances to show how boys and girls are treated differently and how adult expectations of them differ.) Do the children have any similar experiences?

- Ask the children to work in pairs to discuss the question: *How might the story have been different if it was set on a weekend, or when Bill was away on holiday?* After 5–10 minutes, draw the class together to share and discuss their ideas.

- Still in their pairs, ask children to now consider what the scenes outside school add to the story, such as Bill's encounters with Mean Malcolm, the old lady and his parents.

5. The dress with no pockets

Objective

To identify main ideas from more than one paragraph and summarise them.

What you need

Copy of *Bill's New Frock*, small pieces of card, collection of unbreakable everyday objects.

What to do

- Ensure the children are familiar with Chapter 4 before the lesson.

- Arrange the class into groups of three or four, each with a set of small cards. Allow them 10–15 minutes to devise and write questions and answers on the cards about the book.

- Ask for three or four volunteers to be quiz contestants. They should stand at the front of the class. The groups take turns to ask each contestant one of their questions, ensuring they don't choose a contestant from their group. If they answer the question incorrectly, hand them one of the objects to carry. (If the objects are awkward to hold, the game is more fun.) If they drop their objects, they are eliminated. When all questions have been asked, the winners are those who did not drop anything.

- Read aloud the section in Chapter 4 where Bill discovers his dress has no pockets, from 'Pockets?' to 'How *can* you?'. Ask: *How would you describe Bill's feelings about his lack of pockets? Do you sympathise?*

- Ask the children to recall what Bill was asked to take to the office (keys, medical forms, bottles of ink, tennis balls). Ask: *Which of these could he have put into a pocket if he had one? Could the adults have helped him? How?*

6. The race

Objective

To identify main ideas drawn from more than one paragraph and summarise them.

What you need

Copies of *Bill's New Frock*, interactive activity 'The race'.

Cross-curricular links

PSHE, PE

What to do

- Ensure the children have read Chapter 6, or arrange them into groups to read it through at the beginning of the lesson.

- Read aloud to the class from Chapter 6, where the girls plan for Paul to win the race, from 'Races aren't nearly so much fun' to 'let him win the race'.

- Draw attention to the fact that it is the girls who make the plan. Ask: *Do you think the author has done this deliberately? Why?* Bill thinks 'But that was girls for you'. Do the children agree?

- Together complete the interactive activity 'The race', to act as a reminder of events.

- Ask: *Why did the girls think it was important for Paul to win the race?* (His disability meant he never won, and they felt that wasn't fair.) Ask: *Was it important for the story to include Paul as a character?* Discuss their thoughts.

- Arrange the class into groups of three or four to discuss Bill's behaviour during the race, allowing them access to copies of the book for reference. Afterwards, share and discuss their feelings. Ask: *Why do you think Bill couldn't bring himself to lose the race? What does the chapter show us about any differences between boys and girls?*

PLOT, CHARACTER & SETTING

7. Mean Malcolm

Objective

To draw inferences such as characters' feelings, thoughts and motives from their actions and justify with evidence.

What you need

Printable page 'Mean Malcolm', copy of *Bill's New Frock*.

Cross-curricular link

PSHE

What to do

- The children need to be familiar with the whole story before the lesson.

- Remind the children about Bill's expectation of being bullied by Malcolm but that Malcolm whistled instead. Ask: *What does this tell us about Malcolm?* (He is a known bully, he is confident and doesn't worry about others' feelings.)

- Read the section in Chapter 7 when Bill meets Malcolm on his way home, from 'The frock was a disaster' to 'corner and saw him'. Ask: *How would Malcolm feel at Bill's unexpected reaction to his whistle? When Malcolm's gang found him sprawled in the rubbish, what do you think their reaction might be? What would Malcolm say? Do you think this experience would make him change? If so, how?*

- Hand out printable page 'Mean Malcolm' for the children to complete independently.

Differentiation

Support: Allow the children to discuss their ideas with a partner before completing the printable sheet.
Extension: Challenge the children to write the conversation between Malcolm and his gang after they find him in the rubbish.

8. What's the theme?

Objective

To identify themes.

What you need

Photocopiable page 31 'Boys or girls?', scissors.

Cross-curricular link

PSHE

What to do

- This activity can be used at any point in the story. Ask the children if they can identify a theme in the book (gender inequality), asking for examples from the text.

- Hand out photocopiable page 31 'Boys or girls?' and scissors to small, mixed-ability groups of children. Ask them to cut out the statement cards on the sheet, discuss them and arrange them on the table into three categories – boys, girls or both. Allow them 10–15 minutes for this task, then invite groups to pair up and compare and discuss their results.

- Bring the class back together to share their thoughts. Was there broad agreement or were there areas of disagreement?

- Explain that Anne Fine wrote the book after her own children's experiences in a British school, where boys and girls were treated differently, after attending school in the USA, where they were treated equally. Ask: *How might Bill's day have been different if boys and girls had been treated the same at his school?* Do they think boys and girls should be treated equally or should there be differences in some areas?

What do you think?

● Complete these sentence starters.

I think no one noticed that Bill had changed because _____

_____

_____

If people had noticed that Bill had become a girl _____

_____

_____

If the story had been about a girl changing into a boy _____

_____

_____

Because no one noticed he had changed, I think Bill felt _____

_____

_____

● Write the words you would choose to describe Bill's feelings when:

● his mum gave him the frock to wear. _____

_____

● he realised he would have to wear it to school. _____

_____

● he saw Mean Malcolm waiting on the corner. _____

_____

● Mean Malcolm whistled at him. _____

_____

● the old lady helped him cross the road. _____

_____

How did Bill feel?

● Complete the sentences to explain how Bill felt about the things that happened to him.

Bill was embarrassed when

Bill was annoyed when

Bill was dismayed when

Bill was outraged when

Bill was puzzled when

Bill was pleased when

Boys or girls?

● Cut out the statements below. Discuss them in your group and sort them according to whether they are things usually done by girls or boys, or both.

Playing football	Learning country dancing	Doing science experiments
Baking biscuits	Playing with the early years children at playtime	Handing out resources in an art lesson
Helping to tidy the classroom	Reading aloud in assembly	Learning to play the drums
Going camping	Learning how to mend a puncture on a bike	Keeping your bedroom clean and tidy
Moving chairs and tables	Taking messages to the school office	Putting out PE equipment
Singing a solo in the school concert	Dressing up	Skipping

● Compare your results with another group's. Did you make the same decisions?

TALK ABOUT IT

1. Judging by appearances

Objective

To consider and evaluate different viewpoints, attending to and building on the contributions of others.

What you need

Media resource 'People wearing different clothes', range of items from a dressing-up box.

Cross-curricular link

PSHE

What to do

- Invite some children to choose items to wear from the dressing-up box (try to include items such as hats, a hoodie, torn clothing, frilly items). Ask how their chosen clothes make them feel – do they feel different because of the clothes? What sort of character might they be portraying?

- Line the children up facing the class and invite the rest of the class to express opinions about what sort of people are portrayed before them, discussing their various thoughts.

- Display the media resource 'People wearing different clothes'. Allow the children a couple of minutes to look closely at the people portrayed, focusing on what messages their appearance conveys. Invite them to share their observations and opinions, discussing together the various responses.

- Widen the discussion to talk more generally about how people's clothing can suggest something about their personalities. Ask: *Do we feel differently about someone dressed in a uniform, a hoodie, scruffy or sophisticated clothes? Does this really tell us what a person is like?*

2. Should girls and boys be treated the same?

Objective

To participate in debates.

What you need

Media resource 'Boys and girls'.

Cross-curricular links

PSHE, PE

What to do

- Ask the children to think of a football match. Display media resource 'Boys and girls'. Ask: *Is this what you had in mind?* Ask them next to imagine a ballet dancer; then display the image of a girl in a ballet dress. Ask: *Is this what you thought of?* Next display the image of a girl playing football and ask for the children's responses. Then show them the image of a boy ballet dancer. How do they react to this? Ask: *Should there be things that just boys or just girls do?* Discuss their thoughts.

- Arrange the class into groups of six to discuss whether boys and girls should be treated the same or differently.

- After 10–15 minutes, ask for a show of hands – those who think boys and girls should be treated the same and those who think they should be treated differently. Invite one of the groups to put forward their argument for them being treated the same, followed by a second group to put forward the opposing point of view. Each contributor must give their reasons for their opinions.

- After each presentation, open up the floor for discussion, each side questioning the other.

- Conclude with a final vote, allowing the children to change their minds after hearing both sides of the debate.

3. What would Mum and Dad think?

Objective

To participate in improvisations.

What you need

Photocopiable page 35 'What will Mum and Dad say?'.

Cross-curricular link

PSHE

What to do

- Ask the children what they think their parents' reactions might be if they learned their child had misbehaved at school, or shown bravery in a difficult situation (be sensitive to children who may have negative experiences in either area).

- Explain that we see very little of Bill's parents in the story. Can the children remember when they appear? (Right at the start.) Hand out photocopiable page 35 'What will Mum and Dad say?', asking the children to complete it individually, writing their own thoughts about how Bill's parents would react to hearing about the events listed.

- After ten minutes, ask the children to work in pairs to compare and discuss their ideas before using them to improvise a conversation between Mum and Dad about the incidents on the sheet. If possible, pair a girl with a boy.

- When they have completed their improvisations, ask the children to choose the scenario they think they performed the best and rehearse it. Afterwards, invite volunteer pairs to perform their scenes to the class.

- Where more than one example of the same scenario is improvised, compare the different approaches and attitudes portrayed.

4. The fight

Objective

To articulate and justify answers, arguments and opinions.

What you need

Copy of *Bill's New Frock*.

Cross-curricular link

PSHE

What to do

- Remind the children about the fight between Bill and Rohan in Chapter 5, reading from 'Let go of my comic' to 'You *kicked* me!'.

- Arrange the class into six mixed-ability groups, two groups to represent the boys in Bill's class, two for the girls and two groups to represent the teacher. Ask them to work in their roles, discussing the events in the classroom, talking about what they saw and heard, how they feel about Bill and Rohan and their opinions of the whole affair. (Remind them that Bill appears to be a girl in the altercation.) Encourage them to explain to the others what they saw and heard and why they think the fight occurred, as well as their opinion of the events. They may also ask each other questions.

- After ten minutes regroup them, creating new groups including some 'boys', some 'girls' and some 'teachers'. Invite them to discuss their observations and opinions in their new groups, each taking turns to feed back the general views of their original groups. Suggest that the 'teachers' begin the discussion. Remind the children that they should listen politely to one another and contribute effectively. Encourage them to build the discussion, based on each set of contributions.

- Summarise the discussions by inviting representatives from each group to report back to the whole class.

5. Paralympians

Objective

To use spoken language to develop understanding through exploring ideas.

What you need

Media resource 'Disabled athletes', photocopiable page 36 'Researching the Paralympics'.

Cross-curricular link

PE, PSHE, computing

What to do

- Remind the children about Chapter 6, when the girls plan for Paul to win the race. Can they remember why? (He had never won a race because of his disabilities.)

- Ask if they have heard of or seen the Paralympics. Explain that they are sports events designed for people with various disabilities to compete against similarly disabled athletes. Display the media resource 'Disabled athletes' as a stimulus to discuss the difficulties athletes with disabilities face. What are the children's thoughts? What other disabilities can they think of that could prevent people from competing (such as partially sighted or blind athletes, Down's syndrome athletes or cerebral palsy sufferers)?

- Hand out photocopiable page 36 'Researching the Paralympics'. Invite the children to research the Paralympics on the internet under the headings on the sheet. (Further lessons may be needed for this.) Search for suitable internet sites beforehand to suggest to them, in order to save time.

- When their research is complete, arrange the children into groups of 4–6 to compare and summarise their findings and prepare a presentation to the class.

Differentiation

Support: Allow the children to do their research in pairs.
Extension: Challenge the children to do further research into one sport of their choice, recording the information on the back of the sheet.

6. Bill in the hot seat

Objective

To ask relevant questions to extend understanding and knowledge.

What you need

Photocopiable page 37 'Bill in the hot seat'.

What to do

- Ask the children to think about all the things that happened to Bill on the day he spent as a girl.

- Organise the children into mixed-ability pairs, handing each pair photocopiable page 37 'Bill in the hot seat'. Ask them to think of and talk about questions they would like to ask Bill about his day. There are some prompts on the sheet, but encourage them to think of other areas too. As they formulate their questions, ask them to write them on the sheet for later reference.

- After 15–20 minutes, bring the class together and ask for a series of volunteers to take turns to act in role as Bill in the hot seat. Ensure you select children who are confident and articulate performing in role in front of others. Invite the rest of the class to select questions from their sheets to ask Bill. Remind them that questions beginning with 'how', 'why', 'who', 'what', 'when', 'where' and 'which' allow for more interesting answers. Ask them to avoid starting their questions with words such as 'did', 'were', 'was', 'can' and 'would', which require only 'yes' or 'no' responses.

What will Mum and Dad say?

● Here are some of the things that happened to Bill. Imagine his mum and dad heard about them. What might they think? Make some notes of your ideas below and then discuss with a partner.

Bill did his neatest-ever writing, of which he was very proud. But his teacher was not happy, and expected him to be even neater.	
Bill took a bet to kick the football through the school window.	
Bill had a fight with Rohan in the classroom over the comics at wet playtime.	
Because he was wearing the pink frock his mum had given him, Bill was made to sit as the subject in the art class, which made him embarrassed.	
Bill dropped all the things the staff had given him to take to the office, breaking the ink bottles and muddling up the medical forms.	

Researching the Paralympics

● Use this sheet to record what you discover about the Paralympics from searching on the internet. Report back to your group and help prepare a presentation to the class.

	What I found out	Source
Paralympic sports		
Paralympic athletes		
Paralympic competitions		

Bill in the hot seat

● Think about all the things that happened to Bill on the day he turned into a girl. Plan some questions to ask him. You have been given some reminders to help you, but you may also have some ideas of your own. Talk your questions through with your partner before Bill is put in the hot seat.

He became a girl.

Nobody noticed the change in him.

People treated him differently.

He was chosen to be the model in art.

He was asked to lose the race.

He fought Mean Malcolm.

Our questions

GET WRITING

1. Under the weather

To discuss writing similar to that which they are planning to write, in order to understand and learn from its structure, vocabulary and grammar.

What you need

Extract 3, photocopiable page 41 'Weather moods', media resource 'Weather types'.

Cross-curricular link

Geography

What to do

- Display the images from the media resource 'Weather types'. Ask them to suggest words to describe the weather portrayed and how it makes them feel for each photograph.

- Display Extract 3 and read from the beginning up to 'at the very least, quiet'. Can the children see the link between the descriptions of the weather and the teacher's mood, and the effect this has on the class? Some children may like to know this is called pathetic fallacy.

- Hand out photocopiable page 41 'Weather moods', asking the children to complete it as a planning tool. When complete, ask them to choose one weather type and use their ideas to write two descriptive paragraphs – one about the weather and one about any character whose mood is affected by it. This could be themselves if they wish, in which case they should write in the first person.

- Invite children to read out their finished paragraphs or have them written up to include in a class collection for all to share.

Differentiation

Support: Allow the children just to write a description of the weather, leaving out the paragraph about a character affected by it.
Extension: Encourage the children to include a third paragraph, where they describe how the weather and character's mood also affect others.

2. Nothing but pink

Objective

To draft and write by creating settings, characters and plot in narratives.

What you need

Copies of *Bill's New Frock*, photocopiable page 42 'Playscript prompts'.

Cross-curricular link

Art

What to do

- Read aloud the opening of Chapter 3, up to 'while they were painting him'.

- Draw attention to the amount of dialogue and action, suggesting it could be rewritten as a scene from a play. As well as several characters speaking, there is also a lot of movement and opportunity for characters to show their feelings through facial expression.

- Hand out photocopiable page 42 'Playscript prompts' and read through the prompts with the children, ensuring they understand the conventions of playscripts that are being explained. Invite the children to refer to these prompts as they write all or part of the scene in the art class as a playscript.

- Allow the children access to copies of *Bill's New Frock* as they write, but also reassure them that they don't have to repeat the dialogue and action word for word, as long as they represent the scene generally, following the same series of events.

- When complete, suggest groups of children choose the script of one of their group to read and rehearse before performing it to the class.

Differentiation

Support: Allow the children to choose just a small section of the incident to rewrite.
Extension: Encourage the children to include interesting and effective stage directions, including those for actors who have no spoken dialogue.

3. Comic strip

Objective

To draft and write by creating settings, characters and plot in narratives.

What you need

Photocopiable page 43 'My comic strip', coloured pencils, copy of *Bill's New Frock*, selection of children's comics.

Cross-curricular link

Art

What to do

- Remind the children about the fight between Bill and Rohan in Chapter 5, re-reading it if necessary. Draw attention to the fact that the fight was over a comic.

- Hand out the comics you have collected for the children to browse through, focusing on the comic-strip stories. Ask what they notice about how the stories are told – for example, they may be action-packed, have few characters and use a mixture of dialogue in speech bubbles and explanatory storytelling (often underneath the illustrations and usually in block capitals). They may also notice how the illustrations help to tell the story.

- Hand out photocopiable page 43 'My comic strip'. Ask the children to retell the story of the fight in comic-strip form, using the prompts and grid on the sheet. Explain that each picture needs speech bubbles to show what the characters are saying, and an explanatory sentence in the box below.

- You may wish to ask the children to make larger versions of their comic strips for display.

Differentiation

Support: Allow the children to use the prompts on the sheet as their explanatory sentences.
Extension: Encourage the children to include sound-effect bubbles alongside their speech bubbles.

4. A poem about boys and girls

Objective

To compose sentences and rehearse them orally, progressively building a varied and rich vocabulary and an increasing range of sentence structures.

What you need

Printable page 'Poem planning sheet'.

What to do

- Recite to the children the traditional nursery rhyme 'Snips and snails, and puppy dogs' tails, that's what little boys are made of. Sugar and spice and all things nice, that's what little girls are made of.' Invite the children's reactions and discuss their thoughts. Ask: *How does this view of boys and girls link to the themes in Bill's New Frock?*

- Ask the children to write their own rhyming poem about what boys and girls are really like, handing out printable page 'Poem planning sheet' for them to gather their initial ideas. Explain that rhyming poems can be difficult to write, as vocabulary choice is necessarily limited. One way round this is to deliberately choose final words that have easy rhymes to match. Another way is to reword their initial idea.

- When they are ready, they may begin to write their rhyming poems.

- Invite individuals to read their poems aloud to the class when they are finished.

Differentiation

Support: Allow the children to write just one short verse for girls and one for boys. Allow the children to write non-rhyming verses if they wish.
Extension: Encourage the children to write at least two verses for both boys and girls.

5. What next?

Objective
To draft and write by creating settings, characters and plot in narratives.

What you need
Writing materials.

What to do
- Ask the children to recall the incidents that Bill had to deal with on his day as a girl, such as being spoken to and treated differently, taking the bet about the football, posing for the art class, taking things to the school office and the fight with Rohan.

- Invite them to consider what other incidents Anne Fine might have devised for Bill to deal with, and how he might have fared. Ask them to share their ideas.

- Reveal the whiteboard, on which you have previously written this list: 'Riding his bike', 'A science lesson', 'Lunchtime', 'Dining hall', 'PE lesson', 'Music lesson'. Invite the children to have a brief discussion with a partner about the difficulties that might arise for Bill in each of these incidents.

- Ask the children to choose one of the scenarios on the list to write about, in the style of the book. They may use characters they already know, or introduce their own. Encourage them to include both description and dialogue, and ask them to consider Bill's reactions and feelings. Suggest the children begin by making brief notes of the order of events in their chosen scenario, and some of the vocabulary they might use.

Differentiation
Support: Allow the children to omit dialogue if they find this difficult.
Extension: Encourage the children to write at some length, organising their work into paragraphs.

6. Treat us right

Objective
To use simple organisational devices, such as headings and subheadings, in non-narrative material.

What you need
Individual whiteboards.

Cross-curricular link
PSHE

What to do
- Remind the children that the theme of *Bill's New Frock* is about boys and girls not being treated equally – gender inequality. Open a discussion about general expectations of boys and girls – how the two sexes can be the same and how they can differ.

- Ask the children to plan and write a non-fiction piece outlining some of these similarities and differences, and their personal feelings about them. Remind them that a non-fiction piece should have a title and can include subheadings, bullet points and questions.

- Allow them to spend a few minutes talking through their ideas with a partner before making brief notes on individual whiteboards.

- After 5–10 minutes, ask the children to work independently to write their piece, using their notes as guidance.

Differentiation
Support: Suggest subheadings, such as 'How boys and girls are treated the same' or 'How boys and girls are treated differently' or 'What I think', to guide their writing.
Extension: Challenge the children to include ways in which the inequalities they mention could be changed to make them fairer.

Weather moods

- For each of the weather types listed below, write your ideas about the moods they might suggest and words you could use to describe them. An example is given to help you.

Weather type	Mood	Vocabulary
Rain and wind	Feeling fed up, not wanting to go out, bad-tempered	Gloomy, bored, annoyed, muttering, arguing
Bright, frosty morning		
Thunderstorm		
Strong, gusty wind		
Hot, sunny, no breeze		
Foggy		
Hailstorm		

Playscript prompts

- Write a short playscript, using the following prompts as a checklist.

Have you:
- given your scene a title?
- described the setting of the scene?
- written each speaker's name and left a space before the words they speak, like this:

> **Bill:** I can't believe I've changed into a girl!

- given stage directions where necessary, so that the actors know how you want their character's words spoken? For example:

> **Dad** (*sweetly*): You look lovely, Poppet!
>
> **Rohan** (*menacingly*): Hand over that comic.

- given stage directions to guide the actors about facial expressions and movements, such as:

> **Mean Malcolm** (*hands in pockets, leaning against the wall, eyebrows raised; he whistles*)
>
> **Astrid** (*hands on hips, looks annoyed*): It's not fair! Girls are just as strong as boys!

My comic strip

- Use the grid to draw a comic strip of the fight between Bill and Rohan. Include speech bubbles and captions. Here are the key parts of the scene to help you:

Bill refuses to swap comics; Rohan tries to grab it and it tears; Bill punches Rohan; Rohan kicks Bill; they fight; Mrs Collins stops the fight.

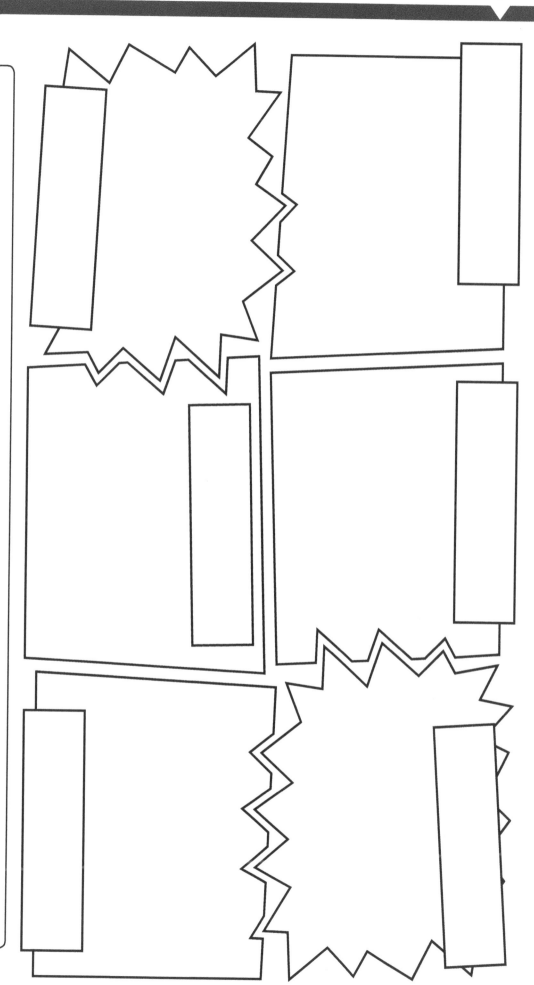

▼ ASSESSMENT

1. Bill's journal

Objective

To organise paragraphs around a theme.

What you need

Copies of *Bill's New Frock*, photocopiable page 47 'Bill's journal'.

What to do

- Ask the children to think about the key things that happened to Bill on his day as a girl – the surprises and difficulties he had and how he felt about them. Invite their suggestions for any incident from the book and Bill's thinking and emotions linked to it.

- Hand out photocopiable page 47 'Bill's journal' and read through it with the children. Explain that you would like them to write Bill's journal for his day as a girl, using the incidents on the sheet. Invite them to jot down their ideas about Bill's feelings on the sheet to use as a guide when they write.

- Allow the children ten minutes to plan, after which they should begin their writing independently. Ask them to use paragraphs for each incident, making nine paragraphs in all. Remind them that as they are writing in role as Bill, they will be using the first person, seeing things through his eyes.

- When assessing the writing, look for correct paragraphing and sentence construction, consistent use of the first person and an effective and appropriate representation of how Bill might have felt in each situation.

Differentiation

Support: Allow the children to select just four or five of the incidents on the list to write about.
Extension: Encourage the children to include some dialogue in their writing. Check that it is correctly punctuated.

2. The story of the dress

Objective

To use simple organisational devices, such as headings and subheadings, in non-narrative material.

What you need

Printable page 'The dress tells the story', copy of *Bill's New Frock*.

What to do

- Ask the children to think about Bill's frilly pink frock. Can anyone describe it from memory? Read aloud to the class the description of the dress at the end of the day in Chapter 7, from 'Bill looked a sight' to 'The frock was a disaster'.

- Hand out printable page 'The dress tells the story', which shows an outline of the dress. Ask the children to draw on the dress the reminders of how it had been affected by the day's events. To help them, read the extract again, asking them to visualise the dress as you read. Explain that they should include an annotation linked to each mark or rip on the dress, with a brief explanation of how it had come about.

- When their annotations are complete, ask the children to use this as a plan to write a more detailed explanation of each mark and rip, suggesting they use subheadings for each one.

- When assessing the work, check that accurate, well-explained reasons are given on the plan and in the writing, that interesting and varied vocabulary has been used and subheadings are evident.

Differentiation

Support: Allow the children to write about just two or three marks or rips.
Extension: Challenge the children to include five or more subheadings in their final piece of writing.

3. Changing attitudes

Objective
To draw inferences such as characters' feelings, thoughts and motives from their actions and justify with evidence.

What you need
Printable page 'What would Bill say?'.

Cross-curricular link
PSHE

What to do
- Ask: *Did Bill choose to spend a day as a girl?* (Agree that he didn't – it was a complete surprise to him.) Ask: *Do you think Bill enjoyed his day?* (Agree that on the whole he didn't.) Ask: *How do we know?* (He was relieved when he turned back to being a boy again.)
- Ask the children to think about what effects his day as a girl might have had on Bill in the future, handing out printable page 'What would Bill say?'. Ask them to complete the sheet independently with their ideas about what Bill might say about the items listed, bearing in mind his experiences. Ask them to consider how his attitudes might have changed. Invite them to write either in the first person, as Bill, or in the third person, as in the original story.
- When assessing their work, look for well-thought-out responses relating to Bill's experiences in the story. Good answers will provide justification for the opinions expressed.

Differentiation
Support: Allow the children to write just one sentence for each item on the list.
Extension: Encourage the children to include two or three responses for each answer, justifying Bill's thinking.

4. Who is Bill?

Objective
To identify main ideas drawn from more than one paragraph and summarise them.

What you need
Writing materials.

Cross-curricular link
PSHE

What to do
- Ask the children to name any of the characters they remember from the story of *Bill's New Frock*. Remind them that these characters do not know that Bill is any different, but some do notice his changed behaviour.
- On the board, write a list of the character names 'Mean Malcolm', 'Mrs Collins', 'the girls who planned the race', 'the boys who played football' and 'Rohan'. Ask the children to consider what each character might say about Bill's behaviour on the day he wore his frock, asking them to write about each of those listed on the board. If you wish, you may elicit oral answers, noting both good and poor answers from the children who respond.
- In their written response, look for answers that accurately reflect the action of the story and relate to the characters as portrayed. For example: Mean Malcolm might have been surprised when Bill walked past when he whistled, but be completely shocked when Bill confronted him later in the day; and the girls who planned for Paul to win the race were probably disgusted at Bill's inability to carry out the plan, thinking him selfish and unfeeling when he beat Paul into second place.

Differentiation
Support: Allow the children to choose two or three of the characters rather than all of them.
Extension: Encourage the children to give several examples for each character.

5. Paragraphs

Objective
To introduce the use of paragraphs as a way to group related material.

What you need
Printable page 'Choosing the right clothes'.

What to do

- Ask the children how the story of *Bill's New Frock* began (with him waking up as a girl and his mum giving him a dress to wear). Talk briefly about the importance of the dress to the story and particularly how Bill found it inappropriate for some of the activities he was involved in.

- Ask the children to think about activities and occasions where the right choice of clothing is important, whether it is practical, such as PE kit or wet-weather wear, or for special occasions such as a party or a wedding.

- Hand out printable page 'Choosing the right clothes', explaining that the children should complete the grid on the page and then use it to write about choosing the right clothes for activities or occasions of their choice. Their writing will need to be organised into paragraphs. Remind them that paragraphs are used to group together similar information in order to make reading easier on the eye and easier to understand. Allow the children to work independently on the printable page.

- Check that the finished writing is organised into coherent paragraphs.

Differentiation
Support: Allow the children to complete half of the grid only, resulting in fewer paragraphs.

6. Speech marks

Objective
To introduce the use of inverted commas to punctuate direct speech.

What you need
Writing materials.

Cross-curricular link
PSHE

What to do

- Ask: *Did Bill tell anyone about what happened to him on the day he wore his frock?* (no) *Ask: Why might that be?* They may suggest he was too embarrassed or thought he wouldn't be believed, or that he just wanted to forget about it. The story concludes at the end of that one day, but ask them to consider that at some time in the future Bill might have decided to share his experiences with a close friend.

- Ask the children to work in pairs, improvising the conversation between Bill and his friend when Bill tells him or her about his day as a girl.

- After 5–10 minutes, bring the class back together and ask the children to choose part of their improvised conversation and write it up, using correct punctuation. Let the children work independently, reassuring them that they don't have to remember every single word, just use the improvisation as a guide.

- The finished writing should use speech marks correctly, as well as other punctuation. Better pieces will also include commas, full stops and perhaps exclamation and question marks. A new line should be used for each new speaker.

Differentiation
Support: Allow the children to simply write the spoken words, without any extra vocabulary such as 'said Bill'.
Extension: Encourage the children to fully punctuate their conversation, using all necessary punctuation and indicating each speaker.

Bill's journal

● Think of how Bill would feel about the things that happened to him when he was a girl, as listed below. Note your ideas and use these to write Bill's journal entry for that one day.

What happened	How Bill would feel
Bill woke up to find he had become a girl.	
Everybody spoke to him and treated him as a girl.	
The boys refused to give him the football so he could take the bet.	
He had to be the model for everyone to paint him in his pink frock in the art class.	
Members of staff gave him things to take to the school office and he dropped them all.	
He fought with Rohan over the comics.	
He won the race after the girls had planned for Paul to win.	
He fought Mean Malcolm on the way home.	
He turned back into a boy.	

SCHOLASTIC

Available in this series:

978-1407-16066-5

978-1407-16053-5

978-1407-16054-2

978-1407-16055-9

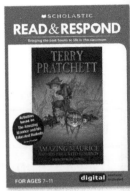
978-1407-16056-6

978-1407-16057-3

978-1407-16058-0

978-1407-16059-7

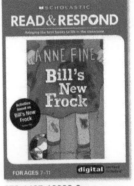
978-1407-16060-3

978-1407-16061-0

978-1407-16062-7

978-1407-16063-4

978-1407-16064-1

978-1407-16065-8 **JAN 2017**

978-1407-16052-8 **JAN 201**

978-1407-16067-2 **JAN 2017**

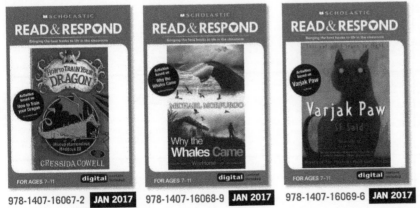 978-1407-16068-9 **JAN 2017**

978-1407-16069-6 **JAN 2017**

978-1407-16070-2 **JAN 2017**

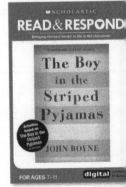
978-1407-16071-9 **JAN 20**

To find out more, call: 0845 6039091
or visit our website www.scholastic.co.uk/readandrespond